BACK TO THE WAR

BACK TO THE WAR

Frank Davey

Talonbooks

Vancouver

Talonbooks
P.O. Box 2076, Vancouver, British Columbia, Canada V6B 3S3
www.talonbooks.com

Typeset in Adobe Garamond and printed and bound in Canada by AGMV Marquis.

First Printing: 2005

The publisher gratefully acknowledges the financial support of the Canada
Council for the Arts; the Government of Canada through the Book Publishing
Industry Development Program; and the Province of British Columbia through
the British Columbia Arts Council for our publishing activities.

Library and Archives Canada Cataloguing in Publication

Davey, Frank, 1940-
    Back to the war / Frank Davey.

Poems.
ISBN 0-88922-514-1

    I. Title.

PS8557.A63B32 2005   C811'.54   C2004-906441-X

for bpNichol and Grant Goodbrand

Acknowledgements

Some parts of this poem have been published in different versions in *Cross-Country*, *Rampike*, *Prism International*, *Writing*, *Sources* (France); in *The New Oxford Anthology of Canadian Verse* (1982), Margaret Atwood, ed., *The Contemporary Canadian Poem Anthology* (1982), George Bowering, ed., *Inside Poetry* (1984), Glen Kirkland and Richard Davies, ed., *The New Wind Has Wings* (1984), Mary Alice Downie and Barbara Robertson, ed., *Relations* (1987), Ken Sherman, ed., *Connections* (1989), Richard Davies and Glen Kirkland, ed., *Copyright Canada* (1990), Alan Dawe and Wayne Tefs, ed., *Thinking Through Your Writing Process* (1990), Judith Barker-Sandbrook, ed., *The Issues Collection: Music* (1993), Kathy Evans, ed., and *On Common Ground* (1994), Jerry George, ed. Three shorter versions of the poem were published in the Coach House Press Manuscript Editions series as *War Poems* in 1979.

Many people have contributed suggestions and responses to the poem: bpNichol, Grant Goodbrand, David Robinson, and many others in the 1970s, and most recently Stephen Adams, Diana Brydon, Melina Baum-Singer, Rubelise da Cunha, Michelle Hartley, Manina Jones, Jessica Schagerl, Karis Shearer, and Kristen Warder. I am grateful to them all.

The function of the Family is the supply of citizens to a community.

—Bronislaw Malinowski

Through this chain of family systems, the fundamental rules that determine our culture are transmitted. We know nothing about it.

—R.D. Laing

1. The Battleship

A small room, faint lines of light
around a blackout curtain. Beyond,

invisible formations of B-24s & Lancasters
drone through the dawn on training missions.

In the colouring book,
the battleship is bow-on & takes up

the whole left-hand page. The nine
15-inch guns are aimed to port

& have just fired. I
am a small boy sitting in his crib

between the world & the ship.
I have coloured the conning tower

green, the forward turret
blue, the deck boards yellow,

& am now scribbling puffs of smoke
at the gun-muzzles, a magic

orange & red. An inch to the right
& where I am not looking

is a black perpendicular line
beyond which the nine projectiles

are already smashing.

2. The Saboteur

Outside the room a white garage,
& behind the garage a gravel lane,

& beyond the lane a thicket of morning
glory & vine maple. Behind the thicket

glimpses of white & brown of the chickens
that belong to a neighbour, the United

Church minister. Over the thicket are the grey
shingles of the roof of his manse,

& beyond the manse
the sounds of a paved road

& the cries of cows at Conway's farm.

On this side of the garage are three greengage
plum trees. The trunks have long splits

in the bark along which clusters of red ants
travel. In the shade of the plum trees

a boy's mother & grandmother sit in wooden deckchairs.
Their boy is about two, & sits

between them, his leather harness tied
to the second plum tree. Beyond the garage

he, I, raise a cloud of dust each time
a car passes down the lane.

3. The Sawdust Truck

I am squatting at the top of the stairs.

It is after the flatbed truck
backs across the grass

to the basement stairwell. After
my father lifts the guardrail of tree limbs
out of its sockets around the stairwell.

After he & the two sawdust men
toss the hundreds of sacks
from the truck, empty them into the sawdust room,

carry them back, folded, to the truck.
It is after. But the truck is not for me,
my mother says, nor the three men

sitting on blocks of wood
in the basement, nor
the red wine they draw from an old barrel that I

have not seen before, nor the barrel,
nor the folded sacks, nor the dust & sweat
on the rolled-up sleeves & dark arms
of the sawdust men.

Likewise I am not for them
nor the painted chairs in the kitchen behind me,
nor the etched flowers on the small glasses
my mother has passed down to them. & my father

who is he for? The sleeves of his workshirt are neatly buttoned.
His amazing winemaker's barrel glistens with cobwebs.

4. The News

"Who are the Japs?" I ask.
"Small & sneaky people," my mother tells me.

"Why does Hitler hate us?" I ask.
"Because he's German," says my grandmother.
"Because he's a Hun," says my mother.

"Who are the Japs?" I ask.
"They bought all our scrap metal
& are shooting it back," my father says.

"How close is Dieppe?" I ask.
"It's over there," my mother says.

"What's a Stuka?
How close is Guadalcanal?
How close is Coventry?" I ask.

"Looks pretty bad," my father says.

"Who are the Japs?" I ask.
"They took our jobs,
& sold us oranges," he says.
"They all wanted to move here
but they couldn't," says my grandmother.

"What's a kamikaze?" I ask.
"What's a Hirohito?
What's a buzz-bomb?"
"You don't want to find out," my mother says.

5. The Mole

The mole comes up through the soil to the rain
& tumbles down the stairwell. Comes up through the grass
across the sidewalk on little pink hands & feet.

It has a black velvet coat
matted by the rain, a pink face, small
pink fingernails. Across its face

is a red furrow. The red
is the colour of blood, the furrow
is the shape of my father's shovel.

6. The Ball

I bounce a ball down the sidewalk
in my own rhythm, my own way.

My father is at work, my mother & grandmother
are talking somewhere inside the house.
& I bounce the ball once
in each square down the sidewalk.

The ball is rubber, is
painted in orange, red
& yellow flames, & the flames
descend from my hand down

to the sidewalk. The sidewalk
runs under a rose arbour, & small black ants
travel on the sidewalk, & the flames
descend from my hand, missing,

nearly missing, not missing.
The ants are running to their homes.
I try not to think of that.
The ants are carrying food

for their families. I try not to.
Instead I play with my dart pistol
& its suction-cup darts. Its range
is three feet & I shoot the darts

across the sidewalk under the arbour

at other ants that travel across the garage's
white wall. I dislike touching the ball
when it returns smudged & sticky

from the sidewalk, & I dislike
looking at the soiled rubber of the dart

when it lies among the yellow
candytuft. One day I throw a green tomato

against the garage wall under the belly
of a stray cat with patches
of bare pink skin on its brown back.
& the cat runs out of my life

& so I bounce my ball once
in each square down the sidewalk.

7. The Christmas Goose

My grandmother is here
just for a while, my mother says.

In the village most of the cars
are parked in driveways & back yards
with sacks wrapped around their tires,
"Until the end of the war," my father says.

My grandmother came with my mother from England
long ago. She gets letters with strange stamps
& stories about bombs that are falling
into basements & kitchens.

Mr. Wahlmann who is building new cupboards
into the walls upstairs for my grandmother's stuff,
drives a motorcycle just like soldiers do
& straps the boards he needs to the sidecar.

My mother calls the year I was born
"The year that Dad died. A Siberial hemorrhage,"
she says. My grandmother
calls it "the year the bombs started."

"It will be good when we can buy turkeys at the store again,"
she says on Christmas Eve as she stands at our kitchen table
& pulls guts & partly digested food from the white goose

that my father has just bought. From a farmer
who came quietly after dark to our back porch.
My mother sits with me & watches.
Or runs to bring her bowls or spoons.

My mother used to be a little girl in England.

"He should have known enough to starve it," my grandmother says,
as she tightly rolls up a section of newspaper &,

lighting it from the sawdust stove, makes a torch
to singe the remains of its feathers.

"The war won't go on much longer,"
my mother says.

8. The Photo Album

My mother has snapshots.

Snapshots of huge ships she calls the *Hood*
& the *Repulse*, at anchor in Vancouver.
1924 she says. Her new box Brownie.
& one of a small freighter
she calls the *Willamette Valley*.

She has a snapshot too of a sailor from that freighter
who she brought home
to her parents for dinner she says
each time it came to port.
The photos are faint & grey.

& the *Hood* was the strongest battleship
in the world, one of ours, she tells me,
looking up from her crochet work
when I ask. & was sunk.
"Just exploded," she says,

"in its first fight the year you were born,
& the *Repulse* was a good battleship too,"
she says, also one of ours,
& was sunk last year by the Japs
with another battleship, the *Prince of Wales*.

I look at her crocheting hands
& at the snapshots, & am puzzled.
The ships were so strong
& have sunk so easily. Their guns
were so big & my mother
is so cheerful as she speaks of their sinking.

The *Willamette Valley*
sailed all over the world, she says,
but never came back to Vancouver

& has probably also been sunk—
in the war.

I've figured it out
that she & my father were married
the year before the war,
that we moved here
from Vancouver that year I was born.

But what if somewhere the little ship is still sailing?
Through seas where battleships explode?
Or what if the sailor is already standing on the dock
& my mother is miles away
living with strangers, smiling
at old snapshots?

9. The Cards

When I get a wart on my finger
my mother dabs it with bleach.

When she gets Christmas cards
she boils the long-spouted kettle on our stove
& steams open the envelopes.

When the milk comes to the back porch
she brings it inside & pulls the cardboard top
out of the bottle, sticks her finger in,
runs it around the rim, then licks her finger.

Then she pours the cream that has risen to the neck of the bottle
into our cream jug.
"It pours more smoothly," she says,
"if you clean the rim."

It's November.
& she has all our Christmas cards & envelopes

from last year spread on the kitchen table.
She has paper clips & small slips of paper
& is clipping one onto each card.
"To tell me who they came from," she says.

She has her bottle of bleach too, & has made
swabs with toothpicks & small balls of cotton.
She is wiping the writing from the cards & envelopes.
"Alice always presses too hard," she complains to my grandmother.

The writing turns brown.
Then disappears.

She steams the stamp off the envelope
& uses the new one to cover the rest of the postmark.

"They don't make good cards any more,
& they're all dear," she says, "because of the war."

Most of the cards are from people like Alice,
in Vancouver, that I've never met.

My grandmother has bought new cards, but has steamed
her old ones open, & given them to my mother. Together
they try to make pairs of similar cards. "Don't
send anything too good," my grandmother tells her.

My mother has bought two packages of Black Cat cigarettes
& is wrapping them in Christmas paper
for the bread man & the milk man.
"They always say thank you," she says.

10. The Drunks

The tram stops at the Coughlan Road station
with its first car
blocking the gravel road.
The Model A comes slowly over the hill on Coughlan Road
round a slight curve, & without changing speed
smashes into the tram beneath my seat.
The glass windshield drops
in chunks into the laps of the man
& woman in the front seat.
The car bounces back about ten feet
& stops. People
rush from the platform to open the doors
& help the man & woman out. Both
are crying loudly, both
bleeding from large cuts
above the knees, the man
bleeding also from another cut
above his right eye.
They do not stop crying
even as they are draped in blankets
& led to the front section
of the tram. My mother
says they are drunk, but I know only
that they are crying.

11. The Boxes

Two galvanized laundry tubs
hanging on the basement wall. Below
two taps at a small sink,
two pink rubber hoses, one
threaded to each tap. Above
three boards make a shelf that hangs
high overhead from the ceiling joists.
Four cardboard boxes on the shelf. Four
small mice & their mother
in one box. One piece of 4 x 4
in my father's hands, my mother tells me.
One piece of 4 x 4 descending into the box—
she demonstrates with her hands three times,
four times, into the box
above our laundry table.

12. The Hotdog

A jelly bean lying on a gravel road.
Gum drops fallen through the cracks
of the wooden sidewalk. "Dirty,"
someone says. & always a second time, "Dirty."

Sometimes I see a candy bar hidden in the grass.
A banana forgotten on a picnic table.
"How do you know who's touched it?"
I hear her say. "Maybe
they'd just been to the bathroom."

After the United Church bake sale,
or the Eastern Star bazaar,
she comes home with a bag of tarts,
or a few cookies, saying
"I really liked the chiffon cake, but
I couldn't find out who made it."

This summer we spend two weeks in a hotel
by the sea at White Rock,
& one day we walk, me mostly on my father's shoulders,
two miles down the railway tracks & through customs
to Blaine. Everywhere in Blaine
are American soldiers & sailors
on leave from the Japanese war. My mother & father
wander from store to store down the main street
& it is hot, & I stand in the doorways
while they look at stuff in the stores,
& in the doorway of a clothing store,
next to a café, a young American sailor
sees me & buys me a hot dog,
& goes on his way, & when my mother comes back out
I have it half eaten, & she grabs it & hurls it,
the white napkin still around it,
into the street under a parked car,

& when she has made me tell her how I got it
she says "You don't take food from strangers."

It is my first hotdog,
& the next week back in the village butcher shop
I see some more hanging in links
from the ceiling & I pull on her arm
& point, & she slaps my hand &
"I don't want to see those things ever again," she says.

13. The Dresses

In Vancouver, at the end
of a two-hour tram ride
is Spencer's bargain basement.
It is the first or second place
my mother & grandmother go,
& there are crowds of ladies' dresses
on racks, & they go to each rack,
& scrape the wire hangers sideways
along the rack-tops. "You already have
lots of dresses," I whine.
"They've brought out new styles,"
says my mother, "shorter,
for the war." The dresses
all seem long to me, & soft,
& crawling underneath I can stroke them
or hug them, or rub my cheeks against them.
Both my mother & grandmother
look for size 10s. While they look
I try to get behind the racks
so they won't shout at me
for touching the dresses.
Once there, I listen for their voices
so I can find my way back if I want to.
"I might like this blue one, or maybe
the polka-dot," my grandmother might be saying.
"Is there another like it?" my mother
is always asking. I like the oval racks best.
I can push into the middle
& be surrounded instantly. The voices
fade, & I can nuzzle the taffeta or wool until
their "Where is he, where is he?"
comes from a distance, or until silence itself
strikes me & I begin wailing
into the folds of empty dresses.

14. The Alley

My mother & I have walked to the egg
candlery to buy rejected eggs & when we
return home there is a soldier, an
officer, just back from Europe & the war,
waiting at the end of our brown chesterfield.
The candlery is in the alley behind the main street
under one of the stores, & I can never figure out
whether this store is Andrews' grocery, or the drug store
or maybe the Glacier Café. My mother & I
walk down the alley, which is wide
& unpaved, pick our way around
the many puddles. All the stores
look the same from the back, although the
eggs we buy are different,
are misshapen, often contain two or three yolks,
& sometimes bloodspots. The soldier
is spotless, in khaki & an officer's
peaked cap, but I can't figure out who he is
except that he's a relative of my mother
& grandmother from somewhere back east
in Regina or Alberta. He is a soldier
back from the war & the back side doesn't look
like the front side. My mother has grey cardboard
egg-flats in her hands, & is surprised,
& I don't think he stays long enough to eat the eggs
& days later I can remember only seeing through the
open door his peaked cap & the back side
of his left shoulder.

15. The Hedges

The hedges have been planted by our neighbour,
the old Englishman, down the back & east side
of our lot. The other side has the rail fence & the dust
of the gravel lane. Some summer weeks my father
punches nail holes into the bottom of a jam can
& pours used motor oil on the gravel
"to keep down the dust," he says. "Stupid drivers,
why can't they slow down?" says my mother.
"Serve them right if they went in the ditch
or slammed together in their own dirt," she says.
"We need a hedge," says my grandmother.

Down the front of the lot is our row of plum trees,
& my father plants forsythia & lilac & snowball bushes
in between. "A little bit of privacy," says my mother.
The hedges are dark green. The back one
has a passage in the middle to which my father
& the neighbour have both planted grassy pathways
through their vegetable gardens. The neighbour
trims the top & his side of the hedge with grass clippers.
The day after, my father goes out & trims his side.
"You should let him do it, it's his hedge,"
my mother tells him.

Some springtimes my father trims his side first,
to be clear for planting, but cuts the top
only as far as the exact centre.
"If he doesn't cut it soon, it will soil the laundry,"
my mother says. My grandmother does all the laundry,
just like she does most of our cooking, but my mother
carries the wet clothes up the basement stairs
& hangs them on a line that runs from the back porch
to a tall cedar tree on the on other side of both the gardens.
Under the hedge, under the laundry,
I like to play war.

I make secret raids into the neighbour's garden.
I roll twigs & pebbles
onto his soil. I aim an imaginary gun
at his cat, his rhubarb, his patch
of Michaelmas daisies.
Sometimes I crawl on a soldier's knees & elbows
to the fence & toss small rocks out onto the gravel
hoping they may knock one of the speeding cars
into a ditch. "They'll have to kill
someone, someone
will have to die," my mother says.

16. The Animals

The black ants carry white bundles
across the sidewalk. The red ants have roadways
on the trunks of the plum trees. The chickens
roost in the apple & cherry trees
of the United Church manse.

"What's that under your cow," I ask.
"Tits," the boy answers, "tits."

The red ants live in cracks
in the bark of the plum trees.
Cracks where the sap
oozes & gels. The chickens
have a chicken house
but roost anyway in the apple & cherry trees.

"What hangs under a cow," I ask.
"You'll find out soon enough,"
my mother says.

Beyond the manse is a farm,
beyond the other neighbours are other farms,
& cows live on the farms
& bellow at sunrise & bedtime,
& dogs live on the farms
& bark as I lie waiting
for sleep.

"What hangs under a cow," I ask.
"Just something or udder," says my father.

I don't get to visit the farms, or peek
into the minister's chicken house.
The cow comes by on its own, with
a boy about 10 leading it, & something large
swinging heavily beneath.

"What's that under your cow," I call, pointing.
"Her tits," he says. "But what is it?" I say.
"Her tits," he says again. "But what?" I say.
"Tits," he yells, "tits, tits, tits!" running now
to keep up with the cow.

17. The Workmen

The pickup truck is parked crookedly in the lane
behind our garage. My father has gone out
to talk to the two men inside,
who are men from work my mother says
& who are drunk she says & probably
want my father to go with them.
There is only the sagging rail fence along the lane,
& she goes out & stands beside it
& tries to talk cheerfully
as if they are invaders who might go away if you're nice.
They are older than my father, I can see,
& need a shave, & are wearing dark work clothes,
like my father's work clothes,
even though it is summertime, & Saturday.
& the one nearest keeps stammering loudly
& has white foam on his lips
& in the stubble around his mouth.
They offer my parents some beer—in clear,
long-neck bottles. My mother shakes her head.

Afterward, my father sits alone on the back porch
& drinks the second bottle.

18. The Tam

My grandmother knits them, maybe for Christmas
or maybe for my fourth birthday that April. Teal green
she calls them. A teal green cardigan,
a teal green tam. I am made to stand
before my mother's vanity, its three-way mirror.
"Looks so smart on him," they say. Then
wearing the teal green tam & sweater
on the tram to Vancouver, being smart
on the straw seats, smart
in the crowds at the Carrall Street station.
At Cambie & 25th they rush across
holding my hands. There's a wind, the tam
comes off, lands on the streetcar tracks. They rush on,
"It's just a hat," they say, as a streetcar rumbles past behind us
leaving the new tam sliced in three.

19. The Brown Bag

My parents' bedroom door opens
into the living room, near the beginning
of a short hallway to the bathroom.
Now & then I notice my mother
rush from the bedroom clutching
a brown paper bag, & trot
down the hallway.

Not real trotting, but taking short fast steps
& staring straight ahead
as if she doesn't want anyone to look at her,
& it always looks like the same bag
smaller than a grocery bag, & soft
& wrinkled from all the trips
up & down the hall.

When my father is there in his armchair
she hurries even more stiffly
& if he calls out
"Goin' someplace, kewpie doll?"
She clutches the bag to her stomach.
"Hee hee hee," my father then laughs.

20. The Toy Planes

The 5¢ to $1 Store has a red & gold signboard
that looks a lot like the signboard
on the Woolworth's store in Vancouver.
It's the busiest store in town.
It has thread & purses & candy & cloth
& knives & toys & pencils & school books.
My little P-40 and Wellington bomber
came from here. My Spitfire. I tug
at my mother's hand. "We have to see
if they have new planes," I say.
I've been hoping for a Lockheed Lightning.
A P-51 Mustang. "The pilots would like
new ones too," my father laughs. My mother
buys me a red plastic Hurricane. "You don't have
one of these," she says. "It's old,
it gets shot down," I say.
"You're lucky they still make toys,"
my mother says. "I want the new ones,
the good ones," I say. "New or old,
they all fly away with money for somebody,
but not for us," my father laughs.
"What are you on about, Ted?" my mother says.

21. The Window

It is a Saturday in early spring. My father
is on his knees on the front lawn before the
east flower border. A burlap sack, its seams
ripped open, is spread on the lawn at his
left side. There are brown leaves, grass,
the stalks of old plants heaped upon it.
My mother & her mother are behind me in the
kitchen. I am kneeling against the back
of the chesterfield behind the glass of the
living room window. The window is behind
& to the left of my father, who is alone,
on his knees, on the front lawn.

On weekdays he does not go out to the garden.
He leaves for work at 7:30 & returns at 5:10
for supper, just before my bedtime. He carries
a dented black lunchbucket & wears large boots,
dusty dark-blue pants, & a dark-blue doeskin jacket
that on weekends hangs high above my reach
in the basement. I listen to him leave for work,
hear him going down the inside basement stairs,
getting his jacket at the landing, walking across
the concrete floor, opening, then slamming,
the outside door, walking up the concrete steps
beneath my window. When I get up I have
breakfast with my mother & my grandmother,
& then lunch with my mother & my grandmother,
& on Sundays my grandmother takes me across the village
to Sunday school. On Sunday afternoons & on Saturdays
they talk together in the kitchen & I kneel at the window
watching my father who is kneeling in his garden.

22. The Airplane

The airplane comes in around 11 o'clock.
My mother is on the back porch
hanging out the wash, a Tuesday
or Wednesday, & I can hear the plane
approaching so loudly that I run out at once
behind her down the back steps.
The cherry tree. Blunt cowlings, turrets,
a two-engine bomber thunders
just above the leaves, disappears
behind the maples up the lane.
I can't move,
keep hearing the roar, seeing
the rows of silver rivets, the fretted
domes at nose & tail. My mother
runs to the basement where my grandmother,
who is becoming deaf, is feeding clothes
through the ringer on the washer
& calls "Would you believe it,
he was right over my head!"
& then runs back outside to where Mrs. Jackson,
our back neighbour, is staring at the sky,
& says to her "What did he think he was doing?—
he was right over my head!" & I wonder that too.
What was he doing, the closest
I have ever seen a warplane outside of the comic strips
& I keep listening, hoping it will come back,
& my mother keeps running back
between my grandmother & people passing
on the road, saying "He was right over my head"
& one time she calls "He scattered the chickens
at Conway's farm," & still later
"Someone thinks he knocked a chimney pot off a house
on Babich Road." But the sky is silent. The reckless
silver flash above the trees
is gone. I don't want it gone.

& when the newspaper comes the next day
& my mother reads in a loud voice
about an air force sergeant who stole a Mitchell
from Sea Island, flew over the valley, & then dove
at full speed into the ocean, I close my eyes
& hear the engines roar again & again
over the cherry tree.

23. Upstairs

Our piano belongs to my grandmother.
Our dining room furniture belongs to my grandmother,
& is bigger & shinier
than my mother's dining room suite which is upstairs
in the sewing room. Most of the furniture upstairs
also belongs to my grandmother, was salvaged
from the big white house she sold the year the *Hood* sank,
the year I was born, the year my grandfather died.
There's a Japanese tea-set she got as a wedding present
from her sailor brother. Two oil paintings
that once hung in her father's pub. A colour print
of Anne Hathaway's cottage. An enlarged photograph
of Cardiff Castle, where she honeymooned. Another of the pier
at Morecambe. A smoking cabinet
which she says was her last gift to my grandfather.
A large brass shell casing, made into a jug
that he brought back from the first war. Two empty
machine-gun belts from his gun. A tall china dog that he won
at the Exhibition. A big tinted photograph
of a red-bearded man & a smiling young woman
who were her parents, & who both died
before she was twenty. The upstairs rooms
are small & dusty, & the wallpapered plaster
badly cracked. I think I am the only one who sometimes
sits in the chairs or looks
at the pictures. Most of the tools
in the basement belonged to my grandfather
& are better than my father's,
but he uses & sometimes breaks them.

24. Supper

We're having supper at the kitchen table.
My grandmother sits across from me,
my father beside me on my left,
my mother at the foot of the table
also on my left, & while we are eating
my father, still in his work clothes,
puts his left hand on my mother's thigh
under her skirt, & says softly
"Hi there, remember me?"
Each time I think that my grandmother
isn't supposed to see, or hear,
& my mother smiles weakly, & says quietly
"Ted, stop it," but then frowns
toward her mother as if to say
"this is not my fault,"
& then my father keeps his hand there
anyway, & moves it again,
& says "Hi there, cutey-pie, remember me?"
It's all he ever says,
& my mother turns pink
trying to both smile at him
& frown to her mother, & her mother
looks embarrassed & grumpy
as if she wishes she were somewhere else
which sometimes I think
might be what my father wants,
& sitting beside him I can see
much more of what is happening
than can my grandmother, & my mother
says sharply, "Go on, Ted,
eat your supper." & all of us
except my father who says
"I'd love to go on"
are quiet for the rest of the meal.

25. The Visit

My mother is carrying an empty black music case
that she used to carry when she was a girl, she says.

We are walking through a hayfield
to a farmhouse on the edge of the village.

That used to be a tennis court, she tells me,
pointing to a patch of brush near the house.

There's two sisters here, she says. One keeps Holsteins.
She points to the fields behind.

The boyfriend of the other sister died last year in the war,
Now she will always have to teach music, she says.

Or help keep cows, I think.
You're a lucky boy, she says.

The front door of the house is double. There are white
pictures of roses scratched into the glass.

The piano teacher is tall & seems young
but also very old.

The house has boards halfway up the walls
& chandeliers of brass & small glass tulips in every room.

The piano is bigger & older than our piano.
The notes vibrate like jars of plums or cherries.

There's a round table beside the piano
with a glass-beaded lamp & a picture of a sailor.

The teacher gives me a book with music
& on each page there's a picture of a very old man.

There's a grammaphone & a pile
of big records made of red glass.

When the teacher gets me a glass of water, there's a humming sound.
They have a well, my mother says.

As we leave, my mother gives her some dollar bills.

You're a lucky boy, we're going to find the money,
she says, when we are walking back to the road.

That was him on the table, she says.

26. The Thunder

The thunder rolls softly behind the mountains & I
begin counting & hoping. Maybe because the thunder
rolls like faint gunfire I have never heard, or promises
to crash like real bombs falling, I hear the rumbling
behind the mountains & begin watching the dark clouds
& counting & hoping. When the rain begins
I rush upstairs to the dormer window
of our sewing room, & watch the droplets
pound & ricochet on the verandah roof & look
across the village below, & the mountains beyond,
for the lightning descending, & hope
for the quick hard concussion of thunder after.
"Don't touch the window," my mother says.
She & my grandmother have always rushed there too,
& are counting off the seconds between lightning & thunder.
They say that it's awful & that they wish it would stop, & they stay
staring till the very end of the storm at how the wet village glistens
in each lightning's flashing. My father is never there,
he drives truck for the hydro company & is usually
out in the storm, somewhere in the hills,
& I picture him kneeling in his black rain gear
splicing wire, or leaning against the dark red truck
to haul shattered transformers from pole-top
with block & tackle. I imagine thunderbolts
striking the ground, fractured tree limbs
crashing, sparks blazing at his feet among
the rebounding raindrops. If I don't imagine,
I will hear my mother beside me reciting her lightning stories.
Lightning that hits the transformer outside & will race
down the wires into our house. Lightning that came in
Mrs. Macbeth's window up the street & knocked
an iron from her hand. Lightning that hit a house
on Babich Road & came down the eaves to a window,
crossed the sill & struck a fountain pen
from a man writing at a table. "It's awful,"

she says. "Terrible," my grandmother agrees.
& the rain smashes down, & all our eyes
are out the sewing-room window
waiting for lightning bolts
& the houses & power lines
bursting & flaming.

27. The Field

The photo in today's paper looks a bit like a field
being cleaned up for building something

except what the small bulldozer is pushing
is people.

It could be a big bulldozer. I'm not sure.
The photo's taken from so far back that first

I think it's pushing long rows of whitish rubble
maybe for a foundation.

The people have to be dead.

I usually like war pictures but I never know
if anyone else does.

Most times they are like my colouring book
a burned tank, a ship, a couple of men in life jackets,
a broken wall, a soldier with a flag.

Most times the photographer wants to get close.

The printing here says "camp" and "victim."

The bulldozer looks very small. & lonely.

I could ask my mother but she might stop me
from looking.

My grandmother would say it was awful.

The dead people all look the same,
maybe because they are dead,
& are heaped far past the bulldozer.

If they were broken stones or bricks there'd be enough
for a castle or a village.

If the bulldozer didn't crush them my father would say.

28. The Locks

A Yale lock on the front door.
Three lag bolts on the basement door.
Four iron bars across each basement window.
One bolt on the back door,
a large spring catch with white rubber rollers
at the top of the front & back screen doors.
There are gates across the opening
of the back porch & the front porch,
& hooks & eyes to close each of them.
There are blackout curtains hung on white string
across every window. When I go to bed
I want the blackout curtain drawn,
the drapes closed, but my door
half-open, & a pine-tree shape of light
to be cast through the opening onto the ceiling.
On VJ-Day I am on the front porch
& the gate is closed, & the air-raid siren
in the village wails for the first time
in the whole war, & only to say the war
is over, but I don't know the war is over,
the siren sounds like war & the gate
is closed, & I run to the door & the Yale lock
is locked, & I bang my fists
on the locked door & no one can hear
because the siren sounds like war, & the screen door
comes closed behind me, & I crouch between the locks
shouting & calling until the siren stops
& my mother unlocks the door & laughs & says
"It's okay the war is over." & I go inside
& everything is still the same
& when I go to bed that night
I want the blackout curtain drawn & drapes
closed, the door half-open, & a pine-tree
shape of light to shine across my ceiling.

29. The Chords

On the piano my mother sometimes plays
"Down the River of Golden Dreams"
& maybe once a year "The Old Rugged Cross."

When she plays "Down the River of Golden Dreams"
she plays the left hand all the way through
as a B-flat chord, banging the notes really hard
when they clash with the melody
at the river's end.

"It's my neuralgia," she says.
"Makes my hands all stiff," she says.

30. The Compost Pile

The compost pile is a large mound
at the base of our cherry tree.
The old Englishman next door
makes his compost in large wooden bins
that he's built in removable sections
—bins for leaves, bins for kitchen refuse, bins
for new compost, year-old compost,
ready-to-use compost.

Our compost pile receives everything—leaves
from our walnut & maple trees,
the rotting carrots & beets
we dig up each spring, flower clippings,
cucumber vines, bean vines, potato peelings,
tea bags, mouldy cheese, sprouting potatoes, egg shells,
pork chop bones, & the roots of the cherry tree
that rises seventy feet above it.

My mother gathers our kitchen scraps in a cracked
green plastic bowl. She's repaired the crack
with a narrow strip of doctor's tape.

The tree is neither a Byng nor a Queen Anne
says my father, but is maybe a cross between them.

When the green bowl starts to smell, or overflow
onto the counter, my mother hustles it out & dumps it
on the front corner of the pile
where birds then gather & maybe
mice & moles too I wonder.

The old man's cherry trees are both Byngs,
small young trees with large black fruit
that partly overhang our lot & that my mother
keeps telling me not to pick.

When I dig in our compost pile
I turn up knots of writhing red earthworms,
anonymously wet, embracing.

The closest I come to the old man's trees
is when he invites me to watch him prune them
with long sheers that have shiny
mahogany handles, or to watch him move compost
from bin to bin, or divide the bedding plants he has grown
beside the bins in cold frames
he's made up from old storm windows.

In our lot, the cherries are smaller, & never get black
& do my mother & father enjoy them, I wonder,
when they eat them?

Standing on the compost pile
helps me reach the higher cherries,
& many mornings I play there alone,
eating three or four, thinking them as usual
vaguely sour, & throwing many more
at the robins who keep feasting
in the high branches on what I imagine
are the only black, fat, & sweet cherries
on the tree. Some years

my father comes out in the evening with a handsaw,
climbs up & cuts off one of the high branches
& its cherries are also sour, & the tree
has an ugly scar where the branch has been
& afterward he flings the remains of the branch
onto the compost pile.

31. The Bomber

It's visitors day at the air base
because there's no more war. My mother
& father & I walk down the hill
to a dark blue bus. Out the windows
we see fields & cows.
Then towers & soldiers.
I stay close to my father.
There are a lot of white buildings
all the same shape. Too many
straight roads. Too many rows
of shining bombers still waiting
to fly off to war. We walk
beneath the quilted metal wings,
beside the bottoms of the tires,
under the marvellous guns & the tall
propellers. Before we have to leave
my father lifts me on his shoulders & up
through the hatch on the bottom
of a Liberator. It is very dark.
Only a faint light far ahead
through the front windows.
A path of slats on the floor.
The sides—just raw metal.
There should be more, I want to see,
or more light, but no one
is supposed to go inside my father says.
When he brings me down
the air explodes with light
& I can hardly see the white buildings
or look high up at the rows of shining planes.

32. The Shopping List

All the way down the hill I've been sent
with the shopping list.
I go two blocks down the wooden sidewalk
to the railway tracks, one block
along the cement sidewalk to the main street
& Modern Market. What's on the list?
Some butter, some flour, some
ordinary things my mother & grandmother
have run short of in the kitchen.
But as I come out of the store
the bag is heavier, much much heavier,
than I'd thought it would be.

Across the sidestreet there's a man yelling—
two horses & their wagon
are walking away, driverless,
from the Buckerfield's feed & grain.
A chance to rest.
I pretend to watch.
I'm about thirty feet
from the store.
The bag is terribly heavier
than I'd thought.
I try again. I find I can carry it
about twenty feet
before I need to rest. So I carry it
& rest. At each rest stop
I sit resting & thinking.
One of the things I think about

is that a big person would know easily
how much groceries like these
would weigh, & that my mother might figure it out
at any moment, & come running to rescue
the groceries & me.

Another thing I think about
is that I don't want her to come & rescue me
& especially don't want the people on the street
to know my bag is too heavy
for me to carry, so each time I rest
I pretend to be loafing,
pretend to be playing with sticks or scraps of paper
on the sidewalk, which is what I've been told that lazy boys
might do & what therefore the people here
might think it natural for me to do.

When carrying the bag, I do less thinking,
mostly thinking that I really would like
my mother to come & rescue me,
& as time goes by
& I am halfway home,
near the Sands house,
& resting again,
I begin to think that my mother
even if she can't figure out
the weight of the groceries
might come looking anyway
since I'm taking so long to return.

From the Sands house the road goes uphill
in two stages.
My mother still does not come,
& I keep on walking,
twenty feet at a time,
up the first rise, & onto the second.
I begin to hope
even when carrying the bag
that she not come,
that somehow I will manage,
I will stagger over the brow of the hill

& in one final rush
stumble through the last fifty feet
to our plum trees, & then
like the triumphant tortoise
carry the crushed brown bag into the house.

Not to be.
Just about thirty feet short of the top of the hill
my mother appears. Unfortunately
I am just then sagging to a halt
after one of my rushes,
so I can't know
if she really has figured out the weight of the bag
or is only discovering it on seeing my knees crumple.
I am not glad to see her.
I know at once there is no credit
in carrying a bag of groceries almost
home. Her laughing apologies are not credit,
& as I follow her up the road
what really begins to worry me
is that perhaps she's known the weight
all along, & has been planning to meet me
laughing, just below the hilltop.

33. The Ship

When he was fifteen my father
sailed as a cabin boy, or maybe a steward
on *The Empress of Asia.* It is a story
I am always wanting to hear,
a story never properly
told, its only narration
coming in minor additions
to other stories, in random
years. Or in images—a photo
of my father in a sailor's uniform
before unidentified water. A profile
that he chalks on my basement blackboard
"*The Empress of Asia,*" "crow's nest,"
"25 knots," "29,000 tons." It is my mother's
tales that make him cabin boy. In my father's
junior steward. In each
he sails from Vancouver on two voyages—
Yokohama, Nagasaki, Hong Kong—1925.
That's all. Had it been a summer job?
Within a year he was a construction labourer.
Later a plumber's apprentice, a shoe-repairman's
assistant. *The Empress of Asia*
has been sunk by Jap airplanes at Singapore.
Nagasaki destroyed by our A-bomb
just last year. When the bombs were falling
my mother & grandmother would have been talking,
my father would have been at work, or in the garden,
or sitting on the chesterfield listening
to *The Shadow* or *Charlie Chan.*
Where is the empress that *The Empress of Asia*
was named for, I sometimes wonder.
Could she have found him a better job?
Did she have princesses?

34. Wishes

I wish it was Sunday, I say.
I wish it was summer, I say.
I wish it was Christmas, I say.
You'll wish your life away,
my mother says.

I dreamed a big machine was chasing me, I say.
I dreamed I was all alone.
I dreamed I was stuck on something
& couldn't get off, I say.
Dreams are just pretend, my mother says.

I wish it was my birthday, I say.
& it is. My father gives me an iron bicycle
that had been broken in half & welded back together
& I wheel it up & down the sidewalk, under the roses.
I wish we didn't live on a hillside, I say.
I wish there was some place to ride, I say.
I wish there was a sidewalk along the road, I say.

I wish I had someone to play with.
I wish I had a brother or sister, I say.
I wish I had a dog, I say.
Dogs have germs, my mother says.

I dream I am in a desert. I dream
there are German tanks coming straight at me.
I dream the sand is coming straight at me. Dreams
are always the opposite, my mother says.

35. The Boats

The old Englishman next door
builds rowboats & small
motorboats in his basement, & knows
the Latin names of the plants
& bushes that he grows in neat plots
in the vacant lot between his house
& ours. He bought this lot before my father could,
& only for his garden, & he must be
crazy, my mother says, even though
he used to be a notary, must be crazy
to spend hours weeding flowers
in a vacant lot, or to build small boats
that he never sails & that sometimes
lie for years under tarps
between the daphne & cotoneasters.
The old man grows green grapes as well
in an arbour on that lot,
& my mother says that he is crazy
because everybody knows that grapes
can't grow in BC, & when they do grow
she says they must be hard
& sour. The old man can recite in Latin
from a poet he calls Virgil
but only I know this. He has been
trying to build a special lawnmower,
one with an electric motor
bolted on top
to turn its reel of blades.
I have seen it in his basement.
When he brings it out
& cuts his lawn, spooling a long black cord
between the grape vines & boats & plots of flowers,
I am inside, & my mother says he's crazy,
"He'll run over the cord,
he's gotta be nuts,

he'll get a shock & kill himself."
& he builds a special shed beside his house
for the mower, & each week my mother
rushes to our kitchen window
whenever she hears the motor stop.

36. The Bath

"I don't love you any more," I pout.
"As long as you don't love me any less," my mother says.

I'm in the bathtub.
"Don't worry," my mother says,
"I was the first one to see you
in your birthday suit."
She pushes the plastic battleships
out of the way & pulls back
my foreskin. "Got to keep it clean," she says.

"I don't love you any more," I say.
"As long as you don't love me any less," she says.
"No! I mean I don't love you any longer," I shout.
"As long as you don't love me any shorter," she says.

37. The Caution

"Never put money or toys in your mouth,"
my mother is saying. She has just walked me
down to the schoolhouse to start school.
I am looking around & can see
that I am the only boy in short pants.
My mother isn't looking around. "Don't touch
anyone's pencils, erasers, or marbles," she is saying.
"You don't know where they've been."

When she walks me back home
at the end of the morning
I complain again about the pants.
"Their parents aren't like us," she is saying.
"They don't care about things, their kids
are left to god & providence, left
to roam the streets, left to their own
devices, not like you," she says.

She walks me down again the next morning.
"See, all the boys are wearing jeans," I tell her.
"Look at them playing in the dirt," she says.
"They look like ragamuffins, they look like
they haven't had a bath in weeks,
they look like they have to dress themselves,
it's a wonder they have shoes," she says.

The next week I get to walk on my own.
"But I need long pants," I say.
"Remember, don't ever eat their food," she is saying.
"You could get sick," she is saying.
"Impetigo or lice or worse," she says.
I catch measles anyway. "That's what happens
when you go to school," she says.
"They're not like us," she says.

While I am sick my grandmother
goes downtown on her own
& buys me two pair of long twill pants.
My mother keeps me in bed for two weeks,
keeps the blackout curtain & drapes pulled.
"If you look at the light
you'll go blind," she says.
"You're safe in here," she says.

38. The Trumpet

The trumpet lies in a brown leather case
in the basement, behind the paint cans
under the work bench. The trumpet
is really a cornet, & is silver,
& my father takes it out of its case,
& sits on the laundry table to play it,
haltingly, only once or twice a year. "Don't
bring that thing up here," my mother would call
down the stairs after the first few notes.
If he tries a song, usually "Charmaine,"
she calls "Watch your teeth, Ted—
don't crack your plate!" He doesn't stop right away,
but looks more pained, & at the end of the song
blows water out of a small valve below the bell
& lays the trumpet, still gleaming,
back in its case.

The teeth my mother calls about
are four false ones that replaced
four others knocked out by a wrench
that had fallen from the top of a hydro pole
before I was born. "That trumpet," she says
is "something else"—"that awful thing"
she calls it to my grandmother
in the same voice she uses to speak of
my father's brother, his parents, their two
cramped houses in the city.
Something else to me, too, squatting
beside him every time he plays.
When had he really played it?
It looks expensive—why had he bought it?
What is he thinking of as he buckles
the leather case & shoves it
back behind the paint cans?

39. The Accident

It's recess, a sunny morning.
We play ride the stumps
in the schoolyard. Some of us insist
the stump is a horse, others
that it is a truck or the turret
of a tank. Perry
sneaks up behind me on the stump
& takes a paper from my pocket.
I run after him but only get winded
and angry. There's a piece of broken English china
in the dirt & so I pick it up & throw it
sidearm. It arcs perfectly, invisibly,
slices into his forehead just over
the eyes. I race to the schoolhouse
thinking I need to be the first to tell.
"I hit Perry & he's bleeding,"
I say to elderly Miss Chappell.
She runs to him, & soon someone comes
& takes him to the hospital.
The class resumes. Perry comes back
the next day with five stitches.
& no one seems to remember the china,
or my throw, or that I'd been riding a tank
across the screaming schoolyard.

40. The Tree

Once again Santa's elves have put up our Christmas tree
& it has the same frosted glass balls as last year
& the same coloured lights shaped like
Santa Claus & flower buds & bunches of grapes.

"They belonged to your grandmother," my mother says.
If one burns out, she ties a string around its base
& hangs it like an ornament.

My dad cuts our tree in the forest
with the other guys on his line gang
& carries it home from the line room.

In each doorway the elves hang
large red paper bells that fold
like accordions. "We got them at a dance
before we were married," my mother says.

"How do the elves find our tree, how
do they know where we keep the bells?" I ask.
"They just do," my mother says.

This year there are new Christmas lights
in the 5¢ to $1 Store window. Bubble lights,
halo lights, plastic angels. My mother buys some.

But there are no lights like our old ones.
"These are the latest thing," says my mother.
"Lots of new plastics created for the war," says my father.
"I wonder what they will have next year," says my mother.

41. Grandad

My father's dad is dying.

I can't remember seeing him before.

My mother, father & I go together to Vancouver on the tram.

I can't remember doing this before.

I have a silver teaspoon at home that's engraved
"Grandad to Paul."

We go for a long time on a streetcar.

My father has a blue Big Ben alarm clock
he bought before the war
when he got his first steady job.

It has a large dent on one side.

We walk past my father's elementary school.

We go to a small house that sits high on its wooden basement
like a mushroom.

The neighbour's house has ragged blankets
covering its broken side windows.

His dad threw the clock at him when he left home
to get married.

He wouldn't let him take his tools either.

"Just the shirt on his back," my mother says.

I'm not supposed to talk to my grandad's housekeeper
because my father's brother has been doing something with her.

The brown church my father's mother used to clean
is across the street.

My father once told me a story about his dad
accidentally pouring tea into the sugar bowl & then
not having any sugar for a couple of weeks.

My grandad is lying in a small bed in a small room we have trouble
squeezing into.

My father is telling him about the weather.

"He was mad because your father was the only one working,"
my mother said.

My grandad had a mischievous sister named Aunt Lizzie
who used to visit this house
but she is lost or dead or missing.

My father once told me a story about his father hardboiling eggs
so they could be cut in half. He laughed.

My father is telling him about his work.

My grandad has thin grey hair on a large head.
He has a big nose & big hands. He doesn't smile.

Will he suddenly jump up? I wonder.
I wish I was near the door. Will he stagger up
& fall on someone?

We are going down the front steps.
"Lock, stock, & barrel," says my mother.
"You mark my words."

"What?" says my father.
"He's leaving every stick to your brother," she says.

42. The Fish

The village lies between the mountains
at the head of a huge lake
that was drained just before the war.
Rainswamp, cat-tails,
cottonwood, birch, & cedar. Sloughs
of brown water pocked with raindrops,
catfish. Standing in black rubber
coats & hats my father & I
catch 47 in two hours.
He cleans them at home, where they are black
on the wet grass, & where my mother stands
invisible. He nails each one
through the head to a gray plank,
then skins it with his electrician's
pliers. There are two hammer blows
to a fish, & later in the kitchen
there are four pink fillets
floating in each Mason jar.

43. The Wooden Sidewalk

"Is a cement sidewalk better?" I ask.
Our village is tearing up our wooden one
& replacing it with cement.
My father looks up & laughs, & tells me
that when he was young in Vancouver
all the sidewalks were made of wood.
"Me & the other boys,"
he says, "used to like to lie under them
& try to look up through the boards, y'know,
at the girls & women in their skirts.
Never saw much," he says
a little sadly.

Later I can't remember where we are
when he says this. Are we walking on a sidewalk?
Are we in the garden, maybe looking up
to watch the Jones girl
trot by on her gorgeous horse?

44. The Blood

"Dr. McLeod has shot himself," my mother says.
"Where did you hear that?" asks my grandmother.
"It's all over town," says my mother.
"It happened yesterday. He left a sponge
in a patient & she died."
"Who was that?" asks my grandmother.
"I haven't heard," says my mother.

"Dr. McLeod really did shoot himself," my mother says.
"Where'd he get the gun?" my grandmother asks.
"It was just a shotgun," says my mother.
"Made an awful mess, there was blood
all over the place, he should have thought of that,
that's what I'd have told him," she says.
"So now there's only one doctor," my grandmother says.

"They haven't been able to sell the house," my mother says.
"What house?" asks my grandmother.
"The McLeod house. Nobody wants
to touch it. They couldn't get the blood
out of the floor."
"Couldn't they replace the floor?" asks my grandmother.

"Somebody's bought the McLeod house," my mother says.
"Who's that," asks my grandmother.
"I'll bet they're from out of town," my mother says.
"Boy, won't they be surprised
when they talk to the neighbours.
Bet they sell again real quick, believe you me."
"You think so?" says my grandmother.

"I couldn't sleep there if it was me," says my mother.
"You can't keep a thing like that quiet,
they should have torn it down,
there's no way I'd buy it, that's what I'd have said.

Every time I walked into that room
I'd see him lying there."
"Is there a new doctor?" asks my grandmother.

45. The Gun

The gun is long & heavy, & is,
my father tells me, a Lee-Enfield.
It's the gun in my old colouring book, the one
blazoned there against a background of barbed wire,
tanks mired in muddy trenches, a distant city
burning. I am excited,
& is he excited, lying on his stomach like a soldier
on the brown living room rug to hold it?
There is army wood all around the barrel
& light brown oil from around the trigger
smudged on his hands.

The gun has just arrived. From the war,
I think, has been brought as a gift
by his mother, on the tram from Vancouver.
My mother is somewhere in the room too
& is angry, she does not want the gun. My father
is with me on the floor,
aiming it into the dining room.
In my head bullets are already racing
between the legs of our dining room table
back to the war.

46. Fires

Where do the fires come from?
From overheated chimneys, from plugged
sawdust hoppers, from wet sawdust, from cigarettes
dropped down chesterfields, from drunks
who overheat the chimneys, & drop the cigarettes
down chesterfields, my mother says.
The firemen are volunteers. The air-raid siren
on top of the schoolhouse rings, & they rush
from their homes or their jobs to the firehall.
My mother & grandmother rush
upstairs to the sewing room.
"Do you see anything," they say.
"Maybe it's only a chimney fire," they say.

The Tamar house burns on Christmas Eve, 1946.
Just after supper. It's the same shape
as our house. We can see the glow
from the kitchen window. "All their Christmas presents,"
I say. "Probably started in the Christmas tree,"
my father says. "Maybe
they're all drunk," my mother says.

Abbotsford Motors burns just after 1,
in '48 or '49. I am at school, just a few boards
below the siren. Jeremy
is in my class, & we stand with him
on the fire escape, with the siren
still ringing, & the smoke & flames
already shooting up in a huge funnel
two blocks away. "Couldn't
be your dad's place,"
some of us yell at him.
"They'll put it out real quick,"
some of us yell at him.

The McDonald house?—it burns late at night.
I hear the siren in my sleep, & try
to keep sleeping. I see Mr. McDonald
all the next week walking in the village unshaven,
his hands bandaged to the elbows.

On Boxing Day of '46 we had walked down the hill
to look at the shell of the Tamar house. At the charred fridge,
the bedsprings, the east wall that still rose
its one & one-half stories. "That's where the baby was,"
my mother says, pointing to the upstairs window.
"The firemen kept hosing that window
trying to save the baby."

"I wish you were dead," I sometimes say.
"Never say that," my mother exclaims.
"What if it happened?
How would you feel?" she says.

The McDonald girls are dead. If I look,
I can see their black shadows
on the yellow siding above their windows.
My mother had run up the stairs as usual
to the sewing room. "Must be the drug store,"
she had called. "Or Mac & Mac's," she called.
"No, it's the McDonald house," she said.
"Look at it burn."

Abbotsford Motors is rebuilt
but goes out of business the next year.
Jeremy's parents divorce. Leave town.
The McDonald house is demolished.
The Tamar house is rebuilt, exactly as it had been.
& the Tamars live in it,
the house with the dead baby's window.

"Don't make faces," my mother had said.
"What if God makes it stay that way,"
she had said.

Sometimes at night I can see the Tamar house burning.
I'm lying in bed, trying to sleep,
& can see the house, & it is not
the Tamar house, it is our house,
it has a radio antenna stretched
from eave to eave, & under the wire there are small flames
on the shingles. I try to think instead
of sailing ships, of black horses, of castles
on green mountains, but each
catches fire, or the house,
a funnel of smoke & flame rises.
I sit up, turn on my light.
"What's the matter," my mother might call.
"A bad dream," I say,
"the house was burning."
"Oh go to sleep," she says.
"Dreams never come true," she says.

47. The Piano

I sit on the edge
of the dining room, almost
in the living room where my parents,
my grandmother, & the visitors
sit knee to knee along the chesterfield & in
the easy chairs. The room is full, & my feet
do not touch the floor, barely
reach the rail across the front
of my seat. "Of course
you will want Paul to play"—words
that jump out from the clatter
of teacups & illnesses. The piano
is huge, unforgettable.
It takes up the whole end wall
of the living room, faces me down
a short corridor of plump
knees, balanced saucers, hitched
trousers. "Well when is
Paul going to play?"
one of them asks. My father says
"Come on, boy, they'd like you
to play for them," & clears
a plate of cake
from the piano bench. I walk between
the knees & sit down
where the cake was, switch on
the fluorescent light
above the music. Right at the first notes
the conversation returns to long tales
of weddings, relatives bombed out
in England, someone's mongoloid
baby. & there I am at the piano.
With no one listening or even
going to listen

unless I hit sour notes, or stumble
to a false ending.
I finish.
Instantly they are back to me. "What a nice
touch he has," someone interrupts herself to say.
"It's the hands," says another,
"it's always the hands, you can tell
by the hands." & so I get up
& hide my fists
in my hands.

48. The DPs

"The DPs are coming," my mother says.
"They'll all be Catholics.
We'll soon be swamped," she says.

"I'm glad there's no Chinese," she says.
"Remember the white slavers in Hogan's Alley?
The ones that got my friend Isabel?
I worry every time I walk from the tram," she says.

"That's because you're too cute," my father says.

There are two cute twin girls in my class
one with long blond hair, one with red.
Our cousin is coming, from Europe they say.
"Must be a DP," my mother says.

There's a big Ukrainian on my father's line gang.
"He was here before the war," my father says.

Two English boys arrive in my class.
They have no father, & live above one of the oldest stores.
They become mysteriously famous when their mother
asks our butcher for a piece of tail.

"Maybe that's what she wanted," my mother says.

The twins' cousin arrives & she is cute too
but has disappointingly brown hair
& speaks ordinary English.
"I just want to feel safe," my mother says.

"The DPs are coming," she says.
"There's enough foreigners around already
just look at all the Mennonites, some days
all you can hear downtown is German."

"They were here ahead of us, sweetie," my father says.

A Dutch boy arrives. He is as cheerful
& tough as the English boys. He wears
short pants & none of us teases him.
His father is a doctor.

"I just want to be able to walk downtown," my mother says.

A Dutch family arrives & opens a small bakery.
They fill the window with strange iced pastries
some filled with almond, some with custard
some with berry crumble.

"They're really good with tea," my grandmother says.
"Their bread's good too," says my mother.

49. The Play

I run down the hill, trip
on a broken board, & end up
in the high-school girl's arms.
I am on the way to grade 2.
& she has soft arms & breasts
& I've skinned my knee & first
she wipes the blood off
& I've been crying
that's how she found me, & I end up
in her arms.

The night I throw up into the toilet
my grandmother stays beside me
with her right hand on my forehead
& her left hand
on the back of my neck. On the hill

it feels even better, the young girl
is warm, I can feel her heart beating
it is amazing, beneath her sweater.

That is the first time I've thrown up.
I'd eaten my favourite meal, poached salmon,
in the dining room of Spencer's Department Store,
in Vancouver. Early in the afternoon
near a window that looked out onto
the boats in the harbour. We'd returned home
on the 5 o'clock tram. I'd been in bed
by 9. I wake up
already vomiting. Wake up
having no word for it & terrified therefore
that I've wet the bed, & call out
"Gramma, Gramma, I've spilled on the bed."
& both my mother & grandmother come,
& my grandmother says, "You've vomited, dear,"

& how good the word sounds, "vomited"—
I do it again in the bathroom, & how good
it feels as she stays there & holds
my forehead & neck in her cool hands.

Tante Anna. Only a year later
I learn to say *Tante Anna.*
This is grade 3, & the high school
needs a small boy to play Johann Sebastian Bach
in their spring play. The role
is to sneak up at night to practice on the clavier,
be beaten by my wicked uncle,
then be comforted by the kindly
Tante Anna. Tante Anna is played
by a girl named Renee, whom I know at once
by her slender arms, soft sweaters, breasts,
by her heart, which sings even more sweetly
than the six minuets which I must mime
on the plywood clavier. & I know
why Johann Sebastian Bach
got up every night to practice,
& why he never feared
his uncle's threats & beatings.

& each day I remember.
Remember running down a hill to skin my knee.
Remember vomiting a poached salmon into my bed.
Remember the clavier, & my wicked uncle,
& the warm heartbeat that waits on a hillside.

50. The Complaint

"Those Gibsons," my mother's lips curl.
"Never have a nickel to rub a dime with—
just drink it away. Never have
two sticks to rub together,
not a pot to piss in," she says,
"it all goes in drink."
She's wearing nylons & a skirt
but only a white brassiere on top
& has the linen handkerchief
in which she wraps her money
open on her dressing table.
"They just live from hand to mouth,"
she says, counting $20 bills.
"It's criminal," she says,
"that's all I can say. They never know
where their next meal is coming from.
He has a good job, but all they have
is the clothes on their backs,
& I'll bet they're not paid for."
It's the day after payday.
My father has brought his cheque home & my mother
has taken it to the bank, deposited some,
& brought the rest home in $20 bills,
& is about to pin them into the white handkerchief
she keeps inside her brassiere.
"If somebody asks them to pay
they just laugh in your face," she says,
"they never had anything
& they don't know what to do with it.
Money just goes through their hands like water," she says.
She divides the bills into two piles,
& puts the smaller into her purse.
The other she begins wrapping.
"When he gets his cheque," she continues,
"he goes straight from the bank

to the beer parlour & she's already there
her glass full & waiting.
It's the kids that get the brunt of it," she says,
now standing in front of the mirror
to pull her brassiere forward, & pin
the money inside. "It's always the kids
that suffer, that's all I
can say," she says. "They sit outside on the curb
& one of them says to me yesterday,
such a polite kid too, he says 'Please Mrs. Jarvis
could you ask my mom to come out & stop drinkin,'
& I said 'I'm sorry Joey, but it would take more than me
to get her out of there,' that's what I said,
but I felt really sorry for him, I did,
& he'll go the same way too,
you mark my words, it's in the blood,
never have a penny to his name, go
from hand to mouth just like the rest of them,
why look at them," she says, snapping the safety pin shut
between her breasts, "not worth the dirt
they were made from."
My grandmother sits on the bed, her arms folded.
"Could you credit it," she says. "How
some people can live," she says. My mother
reaches for her blouse. "It's criminal,
that's the only word for it, someone
should put a stop to it," she says.

51. Sweets

"I could sure be sweet on you,"
my father says, under his breath
as he buys me ju-jubes from Carol
at the candy counter of the Five-to-a-Dollar.
"What was that, Mr. Jarvis?" Carol replies.
My father stammers. "I said you're a real sweetie too,"
he says. She stares.
"I don't mean nothing wrong by it,
you know, it's just that you're a real fine
looking girl, a real nice girl," he says.
"Thank you, Mr. Jarvis," Carol says.

52. The New Car

In 1948 my father buys our first car,
& I secretly call it "Come-on-Steve."
It's a '46 Chev, torpedo-back,
maroon over Hollywood beige.
My father says he's had to pay too much
because of the post-war shortage,
that it had been smashed up once,
& that's why it tops out
at 71 miles-per-hour. My mother
says it had been caught earlier that spring
in the Fraser Valley Flood,
that she'd seen its roof just above water
in pictures in the *Sun* paper, & that strangers
keep stopping her on the street saying "Hey,
you're the lady who's got stuck with the car
that got caught in the Fraser Valley Flood."
Each time she says this my father replies
that he doesn't think so, & my mother
then looks straight ahead & says
that she can only say what she's been told.
This happens a lot, & meanwhile
I sit in the back seat & secretly
call the car Come-on-Steve.
Come-on-Steve is a race horse whose name
I've heard on the radio
on Jack Short's Racing Highlights.
Come-on-Steve is real, is a fast horse,
& I figure could easily have survived
the Fraser Valley Flood.
Steve is Steve Canyon in the Sunday comics
who has won the war & now
flies silver P-51s over China, guns blazing,
& is beloved of the Dragon Lady. "Come-on-Steve,"
I whisper as we drive along the highway.
"Come-on-Steve," hoping my father

will overtake the car ahead.
"Come-on-Steve," hoping he will outdistance
the car behind. All the while
he drives at a level 52 mph down the 50-mile limit highway
towards Vancouver, & my mother quotes
the sworn testimony of strangers on the street,
& my grandmother beside me murmurs,
when she can, "What a fine steady driver
you are, Teddy." "Come-on-Steve," I whisper
nevertheless, & dream the car
will swoop & thunder through the fields & over
the blue mountains.

53. Looking

My father is walking down the main street,
just outside the Marshall Wells hardware.
There is a young woman in front of him
in spike heels & plump
stocking seams. "That's
a cutie," he says.
"Ted," my mother says beside him,
"you're old enough to be her father."
"I'd love to be her father," he says,
shaking his head & grinning.
"Ted, you're awful," my mother says.
"You know I'm just looking, sweetie," he says.
"There's no harm in looking."

In Vancouver, he is driving
past a blonde high-school girl
in bobby sox & tennis shorts,
near the corner of Clark & 19th.
"Hi there, cutie," he says.
"Ted!" my mother says.
"Hey, she heard me," he giggles,
rolling up his window.

54. The Toilet

is at a picnic site
or in a department store
or at a beach.
My mother
tears off 25 or so pieces of toilet paper
to cover the seat
or there is no toilet paper
in the dispenser & three or four
crumpled pieces on the floor
& my mother goes back out
& gets some newspaper
& folds it over the seat,
or there is brown water on the floor
between the door
& the toilet
& she brings in enough newspaper
to lay pieces on the floor
so we can step close enough
to the bowl,
or the floor is only damp
& she has the newspaper with her
in her shopping bag
or in her beach bag
or maybe in the picnic basket
already shaped & cut out
& she arranges it carefully
on the black toilet seat.

55. The Arguments

My father & grandmother are arguing
across the supper table about an election.
"My father voted Conservative," she says.
"The CCF looks out for workers," he says.
"The CCF is always last," she says.

My mother & grandmother & I
are about to take the tram to Vancouver.
My father says he doesn't want to see any more stuff
from the Army & Navy. "It's on the union hot list,"
he tells my grandmother.

My grandmother wants my mother to vote Conservative.
My father wants her to vote CCF.
"You're trying to cancel out my vote," he shouts.

My grandmother has bought an air conditioner for her room.
My father has climbed up our ladder
& installed it. "It's too new-fangled.
It'll run up the light bill," my mother says.

56. Doing the Dishes

"How's my little girl," my father says.
"Go away, I'm mad," my mother says,
& continues washing the dishes.
"It's my favourite little bum," he says,
grabbing her left buttock in his right hand.
"Stop it, can't you see I'm mad," she says.
"A little squeeze'll make you glad," he says,
& picks up a tea towel.

"I don't care, I'm not going back
to the lodge, not after being called a liar,"
she says. "That's what I told
Mrs. High-&-Mighty, & I meant it."
"Aw honey, it's no big thing," he says.
"You just misunderstood her,
it would have been okay if I'd been there," he says.

"Mrs. High-&-Mighty. Some people
think their shit don't stink," she says.
"I said to her 'you better get down on your knees
& apologize, after all Ted Jarvis has done
for this lodge. You have no damn right!'
& you know she just laughed,
just laughed in my face."
"You shouldn't get so angry,
she ain't worth it," my father says.

"That's right, I've got more
in my little finger," my mother says.

"You've got cute little fingers," he says.

57. The Advice

It's summertime. I'm running in large circles on the lawn,
& throwing a ball into the air & jumping
to catch it, & perspiration runs from my hair & down my cheeks,
& my grandmother cries out "Don't get overheated," & when I stop
she comes over & says "You're overheated,"
& goes to get me a wool sweater to wear until I cool off.

Often this is at dusk, after supper, & my grandmother calls this time
"between the lights," like when my father
is driving us home from Vancouver, & it's getting dark, & he says
that he can't see whether the cars that don't have lights on
are coming or going, & she says
"Yes, Teddy, it's between the lights."

What I also love to do is race around the outside of the house
at full speed & burst through the swinging lattice gates
my father has built under the cedar arches at both front corners.
I can hit the gates with both forearms at once, & the gates
explode forward on their spring hinges & thrust me
from shadow into sunlight.

But this always gets me overheated, & if it's early evening
my grandmother calls "The dew is falling, Paul, don't
get overheated." On the highway
my father waits to use the passing lane
to get past the slow cars & trucks in front of him,
& as he squints into the dusk my grandmother says
"You can't be too careful, Teddy, when it's between the lights."

58. Jobs

My father is a hydro company groundman
which is not as good as being a lineman,
but his mother, my mother says,
made him promise not to climb the poles.
His father was a piano tuner in Ontario
& then a meter reader for the hydro company
in Vancouver, & then lost his job,
my mother says.

My father's mother now cleans offices
& I'm supposed to call her "Mimi"
although this is not her name.
She was cleaning a church when my father was three
or four, & when she wouldn't give his father the money
they divorced. She is married now to Uncle Harold,
who is a hospital orderly, except my mother says that maybe
they're not married. My mother herself was a forelady, she says,
of a book bindery, & she got married.

My father's brother plays banjo & guitar in a Vancouver band.
"That is not a good job," my mother says, & my father
agrees. "It's not regular," says my grandmother.
She used to be a telegrapher in Newcastle, in England,
& married a farmer, from Yorkshire,
who later worked at the Rat Portage sawmill in Vancouver,
& then was a soldier at Vimy, & after that did maintenance
at Vancouver schools. "You don't meet good people,"
adds my mother. "& they drink a lot."

My father's brother lives with Eileen,
a Chinese girl. "I don't think they're married either,"
says my mother. We visit Mimi about once a year,
& my father's brother & Eileen are usually there,
& Mimi serves baked cauliflower because my father
likes it, & because he rarely saw her when he was a boy.

I don't know what Eileen's job is, but my father
looks at her a lot, & his brother makes lots of jokes
& sometimes plays a few bars of Tchaikovsky for me
on his ukelele.

Mimi has a grey Pekingese named Hannah, that my mother says is dirty.

My grandmother says she used to bicycle to her job in Newcastle.

My mother says that my father's brother knows better than to bring Eileen
to our place to visit.

My father says that when he was little his brother would secretly walk him
across town to visit Mimi.

My mother tells my grandmother that Mimi is bigger than Harold &
makes him toe the line.

My grandmother says that when my grandfather was in the war at Vimy a
rat fell into her bathtub & she killed it with a piece of firewood.

My mother says that Mimi gives me & my father expensive gifts, like
watches & radios, because she walked out on him when he was young.

My father says Eileen is a cutie.

My mother says that someday his brother will settle down.

His brother jokes that their father was feisty with his fists, or was he fisty
with his feists, he says, & Mimi says nothing, & the rest of us know what a
joker he is.

59. The Pets

All week the verandah is filled
with the ladders, buckets & canvas
of the paperhangers. & a grey & white cat
arrives. It is drinking milk from a saucer
beside the buckets. It climbs
the neighbour's maple tree & is afraid
to come down. I want my father
to get one of our ladders & go after it.
It would make a good pet, I say.
My grandmother says all cats are dirty.
& my mother says it's a female,
that nobody keeps female cats.
When the paperhangers go the cat vanishes.
A year later a stray black Lab
begins to sleep on the verandah
& there are only canvas curtains
to deflect the sun. I take him water,
& get him bones & kitchen scraps
from my grandmother. There is the sound
of his nails on the verandah boards
when he scrambles to his feet
to meet me, of his tail
slapping against the railing.
Then he too vanishes.
"Needed a home in the country," says my grandmother,
some time later. "I'm sure he's fine," says my mother.
"It's a good thing we have the car.
We let him out near some farms," she says.

60. The Lessons

My mother says I can catch a bird
if I put salt on its tail. I go outside
with the shaker. The birds stay away.

My grandmother teaches me Morse code.
Dot-dot-dot dash-dash-dash dot-dot-dot I tap.
No one replies.

My mother says that eating fresh carrots
will help you see in the dark. My father is growing carrots.
"You should take that with a grain of salt," he says.

My teacher says I should write a story.
I write a story about Taiwan.
"What's a Taiwan?" ask the English boys.

I put a long blonde hair from one of twins
into my Bible. Nothing happens.
"It's the wrong hair," my father says.

The church starts a cub scout pack.
There are five of us. We learn to send smoke signals.
To no one.

My father tells us about a lineman who was so pie-eyed
that he threw up from the top of the pole.
"Those kind aren't worth their salt," declares my grandmother.

The clerk in our dry-goods store writes a book of poems.
He calls it *Cloth of Gold* & sells it at the front counter.
"Sells it by the yard, eh?" says my father.

At school I rewrite the story.
I set out to carry it home.
Two big boys from the high school

dot-dot-dot dash-dash-dash dot-dot-dot
tear it into pieces & throw it into the creek.
"It's going to go far," Ron & Kenny say.

My mother hurries down the hill to the creek
to gather the pieces. She finds most of them
& scotchtapes them together but into a different story.

It's supposed to be about Taiwan, I say.
"Did you say 'tie one on'?" asks my father.

61. Water

The nearest water is Mill Lake
which fifty years before had been the pond
for a lumber mill, none of which
shows now above the surface.
There are weeds on the bottom,
pilings too, I suppose,
that once held the mill, & sunken logs
that no one has ever seen
because of the mud that hangs suspended
in the water. There is a small park, & a beach
with a quick drop into the brownness.

Five miles north is the Fraser River,
a half-mile wide, with whirlpools & eddies
& huge logs & tree branches jammed by the current
at violent angles into the bottom.
It has tugboats & gillnetters
but no swimmers, & no record,
my mother likes to say, of survivors
from sudden overboards or sinkings.

Dead Man's Hole is ten miles away to the east,
near the drained lake that is Sumas Prairie. My father
says a man hanged himself there, on horseback,
forty or fifty years ago, from one of the many
cottonwood trees that grow in a ring around it.
The water in the hole is bottomless,
he says. The man had maybe knifed
a woman to death, he thinks,
& thrown the body into the hole.

Never came back, my mother says.
The man's body too had been thrown in the hole,
she adds, & is probably still there. Perhaps,
she says, snagged in the cottonwood roots,

or maybe caught in quicksand.
"You never know," she says. "Maybe
there's a current under the fields
to the Fraser River."

Beyond Sumas Prairie is Cultus Lake,
with a mountain road, a large park,
auto courts, rows of pre-war summer cabins.
At the park is a floating wharf which encloses
a square of water. Cultus, says my mother,
is an Indian word that meant 'death'
or perhaps 'treachery' or even
'bottomless lake'. I like to wander
up the grassy lanes in the grid
of summer cabins & try out
the rusting hand-pumps at the intersections.

Every time someone drowns in Cultus,
my mother says, they drag for the body
but never find it. In the grass one day
I find a cut-glass salt cellar
with a sterling-silver top. Maybe
there's an underground river, she says.
Maybe there's a current that carries them away.
One Sunday I am running, rolling,
& tumbling near the beach on a large public lawn
on which some young men have also
been tumbling & doing shoulder stands,
& I find a 1947 silver dollar, a fifty-cent piece,
a quarter, & three pennies, & when I tell her
my mother says "Shhhh, someone will hear you
& say it's theirs," & all that afternoon
she looks uncomfortable, as if something bad
is waiting in the trees
or out behind her in the lake.

After the war whenever someone drowns
in Mill Lake, the air-raid siren
rings three short blasts.
In truth, when the inhalator is needed anywhere
in the village, the air-raid siren
rings three short blasts. Each time,
my mother says that someone must be drowning
in Mill Lake. "It's the weeds on the bottom,"
she says. "They find the bodies
stuck in rotten logs or tangled
in torn plants." Only twice
does someone drown. In the weekly paper
I look for the police reports.
One boy hit his head on a rock
when he dove into the only shallows,
near the beach. The other got cramps,
the paper says, had just eaten. His body
took three hours to find
because of the muddy water,
the rotting logs, it says, & the weeds
that grow so profusely
on the dark lake bottom.

62. The Victory

"She was yakkin' about Ted.
& I let her have it good," says my mother.
"Who was this?" says my grandmother.
She's starting to scramble some eggs for our lunch.
"Irene. Down at the lodge last night," my mother says.
"I said 'You'll open your mouth once too often,'
that's what I said. She didn't know what
to say. She just stood there with her jaw hanging."
"We'll need more toast," my grandmother says.
"What had she been saying?" she asks.
"Oh you know," says my mother.
She puts some bread in the toaster.
"Stuff about Ted wanting to run everything.
She sure had another think coming."
"You shouldn't take such people seriously," says my grandmother.
"I wasn't going to take that from no one," says my mother.
"'You don't know what you're talking about,
you're just shooting off your mouth,' I said.
You should have seen the look on her face."
My grandmother grabs the toast & begins buttering it.
"She didn't know I was there.
She didn't have a foot to stand on.
She just looked at me," my mother says.
"What did she say then?" says my grandmother.
"What could she say?" says my mother.
"There was nothing she could say.
'Oh I didn't mean it that way,' she said.
'Don't you lie to me,' I said.
'You've already said too much,
You're not going to worm out of this one,' I told her.
I really gave it to her," she says.

63. The Jacket

My father was once hugging my mother
& called her "Louise."
She says that was a long time ago. But if the song
comes on the radio, she turns it off.

In an oval frame she has a small photo
of him, standing near the middle
of a narrow suspension bridge, a footbridge,
over cedar trees, a narrow canyon. The frame
stands on her dresser & matches
her silver mirror & brush set, the photo
is grey & faded, & my father
stands young & smiling
in a casual jacket & light slacks
over a canyon I have never seen.

On our record player he often plays
"Far Away Places," "A Slow Boat to China,"
"Slippin' Around."

I see the jacket all the time. It hangs
on a hook inside our back door
& is never worn except by my mother
on windy days when she leans from the back porch
to pull our washing back
to the house. It's made of tan doeskin
& has brown tweed panels down the chest,
& is now probably too small for my father
but I like to try it on, & each time
it's much too big & my mother says
"It's a horrible old thing,"
yet when I hold it up
there are no holes or tears.

My father usually shaves in his sleeveless undershirt.
He uses a Rolls razor, from England he tells me.
While he is shaving, he often whistles.
"Every little breeze seems to whisper Louise," I sometimes hear.

64. Bears & Hunters

"You'll never guess," my mother says.
My father looks up.
"We heard it at the butchers," she says.
"They've found an old plane on Tiger Mountain,
just over there," she says, pointing
to the nearby mountain that is always marked
by a huge dog- or tiger-shaped patch of snow.
"They know which one it is by the number
on the tail—one of the Liberators
that went missing back in '43.
I knew those boys," she says.
"I used to see them at the Glacier,
I knew something was wrong
when I asked this pilot 'Where's your friends?'
& he looked down & said
'I don't want to talk about it,'" she says.
"Aw Jeannie, it could have been any of them,"
my father says. "The guys you remembered
could have been sent to the war," he says.
"Maybe," she says. "Anyway, when they found this plane
the bones were scattered all over the mountainside."
"By bears," she says. "& they didn't find any wristwatches
or wallets," she says. "Can you imagine hunters
finding the wreck & not reporting it?" she says.
"I just feel sorry for their families," she says.
"The hunters' families?" asks my father.
"No, silly," says my mother. "The boys' families.
How will they feel to know about the bears & the hunters?"
"Unbearable?" asks my father.

65. Hatzic Lake

We drive to a picnic at Hatzic Lake.
We go only this once to Hatzic Lake,
& there is still mud on the lawns
from the Fraser Valley Flood,
& horizontal stains on the walls
of most of the buildings, from the high water.
It's a lodge picnic, the first
Falcons' Picnic, & there are a lot of cars,
even a new Tatra from Czechoslovakia,
& a '49 Ford police car, black & white,
with its siren neatly hidden
in the round centre of its grill.
Near the end of the day Ray Oberlander
gets drunk & backs his new '49 Chev
into the women's outhouse, & knocks it
off its hole. The right rear wheel of the Chev
then slips into the hole, & the outhouse
falls back, mostly upright, onto its rear bumper,
& there is a woman inside the outhouse
screaming—I'm sitting at our picnic table
maybe fifty feet away, & I'm thinking
that Ray Oberlander is the Falcons' president,
& when the woman screams I'm thinking
that if you can't trust the president
of your own lodge not to get drunk
& knock over the outhouse while you're sitting in it,
who can you count on? & Ray Oberlander
is not even admitting he has knocked over the outhouse,
is sitting there revving his motor & spinning his wheel
in the hole, & looking straight ahead
as if nothing special is happening.
But the woman in the outhouse keeps yelling
& about 10 men on the softball diamond
across the lane hear her, & saunter over,
all naked to the waist, & they say

"C'mon Ray, cut the motor,"
& lift the rear wheel out of the hole
& then lift the outhouse
back over the hole. While they are lifting
the outhouse, Ray Oberlander drives away,
& shouldn't he have to pay
for the splintered corner I wonder,
& the woman inside
calls that she is OK, & the men
yell something about a hole, & she laughs back
& they saunter back to their softball game. My mother
doesn't let me swim that day
in Hatzic Lake, or even play
on the beach. It's only one year
since the flood, & there are dead cows
still rotting in the water,
& even the outhouses, she says,
had floated every which way.

66. The Bad Men

"I'm sure glad you're all right," my mother says.
"We sure almost weren't."
I've just got up on Sunday morning.
"We could have been killed, or worse," she says.
I look to my father, who is making himself some porridge.
"When we got home from the dance," she says,
"there was a strange car in the driveway.
We didn't know what to think.
They could have been in the house.
Anything could've been happening," she says.
"It wasn't like that, Jeannie," my father says.
"We could see the windows were all steamed up.
We knew there was someone in the car,
that they'd been there for a while."
"Yeah," says my mother, "& you were all for going
& asking them to move," she says.
"What did you do?" I ask.
"I got your father to turn around
& go down to the police," she says.
"That's what I was going to do," he says.
"It's a good job you did," she says. "They were big guys,
Two of them. Indians. The car was stolen."
"They were big," says my father.
"Not sure they were Indians.
But they gave no trouble," he says.
"A good thing," she says. "There was only one cop,
Van Dusen. He had your father help hold each guy
while he handcuffed them. It was pretty bad," she says.
"They just seemed sleepy," my father smiles.
"That's probably why they'd stopped," he laughs.
"But then you had to ride back down
with them & Van Dusen," she says.
"After we'd checked the house. I was scared,
you're not a cop," she says.

"I didn't have to. He's a friend.
He was on alone," he says.
"He had no right," she says. "It wasn't funny,
you're just lucky," she says.

67. Jeannie Bitch

The phone rings late on a Sunday morning.
My father comes straight from it to my mother
who is folding towels on the dining room table.
"That fire you heard last night," he says,
"It was the Falcons Hall."
"Oh my God," says my mother.
"Not burned to the ground?" she says.
"Gutted the kitchen, smoked most
of everything else," he says.
"That's grim," she says, "that's really grim,"
& marches to the window nearest to downtown
as if hoping to put the fire out.
"I bet they try to blame us," she says.
"What d'you mean, that's stupid," my father says,
"the Brady's & us all left together."
"But you locked up," she says.
"Don't you dare get involved.
They always blame the last one there," she says.
"Will you shut up," he says.
"There you go taking it out on me," she says,
marching back to the table.
"I'm not," he says, "be reasonable, woman,
they're pretty sure it was just a cigarette
someone tossed in the garbage."
"You always blame me," she says,
snatching up the towels one by one & snapping them into folds
as if they were burning. "I'm just Jeannie-bitch
to you. Jeannie-goddamn-bitch," she says.
"C'mon, woman," my father says.
"We don't need this, there's been a fire & they need
all the help they can get to sort out the damage.
No one's blaming you."
He reaches out to put an arm around her.
She shakes it off & hurls
the pile of folded towels to the floor.

"You go to your goddamn lodge.
I know what you think of me," she says.
"I'm just shit to you," she says.
"Shit shit shit!" & runs to their bedroom
& slams the door. My father considers the door.
"Don't say anything to her,"
he says to me as he leaves.

68. The Fall Fair

My mother & I walk along the shoulder of the highway
to the fairgrounds. We go into the barn
& see the sheep & pigs. We see the famous cow, Daisy K.

We go upstairs in the barn to where the gun club meets.
We see the thick bullet-riddled boards at the end.
We see the prize-winning squash, the prize-winning pie,
the prize-winning table cloth.

My mother knits & crochets a lot. This year
she crocheted a large basket
& soaked it in sugar water so that it would stand up
like a real basket, & gave it to the lodge as a door prize.

We see prize-winning woodcarvings
& prize-winning macramé
& prize-winning macaroni art.

In the paper last week I read that Daisy K
is still leading for butterfat production.
I read that Bill Code still tops the standings
at the gun club.

Last year my mother did shell-work for the lodge bazaar.
She bought little plastic plaques & packages
of small sea-shells through the mail & glued the shells
on the plaques so they looked like flowers.
"You could have entered," I tell my mother.

We go outside & see lots of people
tossing coins at dishes, or firing
crooked guns at targets
to try to win stuffed blue bears or pink dogs.
"Those games are all rigged," my mother says.

Last spring she took me by bus across the river
to the Music Festival in Mission
to compete in grade 3 piano. There was a girl there
from New Westminster, called Naomi McCorkindale,
who played the piano with her whole body,

leaning far over the keys, as if trying to feel every note.
"It's not fair to come from so far away," my mother said.
"They have their own festival." & when she beat me by one point,
said, loudly enough for Naomi to hear,
"Looked like she was playing the thing with her nose."

At the fairgrounds there are lots of farm kids my age
looking after animals, or running loose
with money to spend on the rides.
My mother & I go on the Merry-Go-Round
& then on the Tilt-a-Whirl. Then we go to the horse ring early

to get a good seat in the bleachers.
A lot of older people come late, & find the bleachers
are almost full. "We sure showed them," my mother says.
"They should have thought ahead," she says.
"That's what we did," she says.

But then the horse guy in charge bellows for all the kids
to get out of the stands. He's wearing a cowboy hat
& boots. There's yelling & groaning
as the gangs of kids scramble down. "I mean you too,"
the horse guy shouts, pointing at me.

"He's with me," my mother calls.
"I don't care if he's with the queen of England,"
the horse guy replies.
My mother looks stiff & worried.
"I don't take shit from you, Vic Turnbull," she screams.

"You go back to your barn,
go back to your pig pen." A lot of people,
a lot of kids, are laughing. Vic Turnbull laughs too,
and turns away, shaking his head.
"We sure fixed him," she says.

69. The Liar

What message has my piano teacher written
in my music dictation book? Standing beside the piano
my mother & I talk, then argue. All at once
she slaps me across the cheek with the rings
on the back of her left hand.
I can feel blood on my cheek.
"You cut me on purpose," I whine.
"That's nonsense, it was an accident,
You made me do it,"
she says. "That's what you say," I say,
& she gets angrier, & calls my father in
from the garden. "He's calling me a liar again,"
she shouts, "a shitty liar."
My father says I have to apologize,
& I shake my head & point to where she hit me,
& when he hesitates about what to do next
she screams I must be crazy to think she cut me on purpose,
& that crazy people belong in Essondale,
the mental hospital near Vancouver,
& that my father is to change his clothes
so they can take me. & so he does,
putting on dress pants & shirt
& a bolo tie & a brown Harris tweed jacket
while she puts on her nylons, & make-up.
& I sit on the piano bench, worrying hard
about when or if my father is going to take charge
of things. But she puts on her blue straw hat,
& navy blue coat, & tells him
to back the car out of the garage, & he does,
& I remain on the piano bench desperate
to stay coatless, & then she starts
crying & shouting "shit" & "shitty"
& my grandmother comes downstairs
& tries to put an arm around her
& my mother runs & shuts herself in the bedroom

behind the piano, & my grandmother
goes out & gets my father
& they go into the bedroom
& I go to my own room & lie down
& the evening is filled with strange steps & whispers.
"Your mother is a fine woman," my father says
the next morning. We're in the kitchen,
my mother is already up, fixing breakfast
& seeming busily cheerful. "You remember that."
"She just wants you to do well," he says.
I nod my head because she is there,
& looking everywhere but at us.

70. The Christmas Party

"You're looking real good today, Irene,"
my father says to Murray's wife
as the five of us sit together
near the end of the Falcons Christmas party.
She has a strapless dress, dyed
red hair, long burgundy fingernails.
"She don't do it for me," Murray comments,
yawning into his coffee.
"You & I should step out sometime,"
my father says, nodding slyly at Irene
at where her straps would have ended.
"Think you could handle it, eh," Irene
leans back to suck speculatively
on her cigarette. My father shakes his head,
"I could sure give it a try, hee hee hee," he says.
My mother stares down the room at the white dinner jacket
of the accordion player.
"When you wanna try, big boy?" says Irene grinning.
"Hee hee hee, I was only kidding,
I love to kid," he says.
Irene leans forward & butts her cigarette.
"Sure Ted, we all know you, don't we Jeannie?"
My mother looks away. My father laughs.
"You know I don't mean no harm by it," he says.

71. The Eyes

"I couldn't believe my eyes," my mother says.
"Seeing is believing," says my father.

"You can't tell by what they let you see," she says.
"I'd have to look into that," he says.

"Often things aren't what they seem,
you have to have eyes in the back of your head," my mother says.
"I'd like to see that," says my father.

"You've got to read between the lines," says my mother.
"You'll just see what you want to see," says my father.

"There's more there than meets the eye," my mother says.
"I only have eyes for you, honey bunch," my father says.

"There are eyes everywhere," she says.
"Some are real lookers," he says.
"Looks can kill," says my mother.

"You've got to keep your eyes open," she says.
"Yes, you've got to see for yourself," my father says.

"You've got to see through things," she says.
"You mean you've got to see things through?" he says.

"I mean you've got to see through people," my mother says.
"I say the eyes have it," my father says.

"The facts are right before your eyes,
they're staring you in the face," my mother says.
"You're just looking for trouble," my father says.

"That's a real eye-opener," says my mother.
"I see," says my father.

"You don't see nothing," my mother says.
"I see what I see," he says.

"I can read you like a book," says my mother.
"Don't miss the dirty parts," laughs my father.

72. The Joke

It's October, & my mother & grandmother
are beside the front porch, picking chrysanthemums,
& my father is on a ladder by the garage
cutting back the climbing roses for the winter.
He's wearing his work gloves
& one of the Indian sweaters
my mother has knit for him, & suddenly
he straightens up & looks at the yard,
which he's just raked, at the house,
at my mother & grandmother,
who are debating which flowers to pick,
& at our Chevvy in the driveway,
& he says to me, "Look at all this,
haven't I done good," & I nod my head
because I know he expects me to.
"There was a time," he says.
& I wonder if he's thinking
about Louise, or his trumpet,
or maybe about his father's house
and the dented alarm clock. & then
he starts to laugh & says,
"Some day, son, this will all be yours."
He seems to know he's quoting something,
& that makes him laugh more
& he lowers the clippers & slaps his knee.
"Some day," he says, "ho ho"
—he really does say "ho ho"—
"you'll have to be on this ladder."
He comes down & gathers the clippings,
& carries them to where he's piled the leaves
on the compost pile. Then we head back to the garage
to put away the long wooden ladder.
"Won't that be funny," he grins.

73. The Dream

This is the dream I've stopped telling.
I'm in the basement. There are no stairs.

There's a gun & a guitar leaning
in a corner. A lot of rusty tools. Lots
of paint cans & jam cans & sacks
& coils of rope where the stairs should be.
& sometimes when I go into the sawdust room

I'm suddenly in the top of the house,
in my grandmother's rooms, beside the photos
of castles & the picture of crossed flags
& my grandfather in his army uniform
& there are no stairs.

The windows are covered with newspapers
to keep out the cold. There's a dressmaker's
manikin, & a lot of fancy English china
on the table & on top of the old radio & some
broken on the floor, maybe by me.

In this dream I used to call for my mother
but I don't now. I think she's locked up
somewhere too, maybe in the basement
when I'm here, or maybe here
when I'm there.

My grandmother's rooms are very small.
There's a smell of lilac & carnations, & often
when I turn I see my grandfather
standing like a statue in his uniform
where the staircase once was.

The dream doesn't end, it just sort of
locks up, & I'm not in the house at all,
I'm back on the sand dunes in the desert

& in the distance the German tanks
lurch toward me.

They are Tiger tanks of course
& I used to worry about them, but they lurch
so slowly that I now worry more about the sand.
I hate the sand.
I think it wants to be me.

I'd much rather be trapped in the basement,
I'd much rather be trapped in the attic.

74. The Fortune Teller

"I'll never reach 40," my mother says.
"I have a short life-line," she says,
holding out her palm, solemnly
& pointing. "I went to a fortune teller
before the war," she says, "at the Exhibition,
& she took one look at my hand & she gasped
& said 'Oh my dear, I'm so sorry,
you shouldn't have come in here,' & I said
'What is it, can't you tell me?' & she said
'No, I can't bear to tell you,
oh you poor dear,' she said,
& she threw her arms around me
& she hugged me just like that," she says.
"& it was only later," she says,
"that Isabel told me about my life-line."
"It was the same thing," she says,
"with Dr. McCready, he'd be listening to my heart
& a sad look would come over his face,
& he'd put his arms around me & hold me tight
just for a minute, & afterward
he'd smile as if nothing had happened
& say I was okay, but I always knew
what he'd been thinking," she says.
"I always knew," she says.

"What will you do when I'm gone?" she says,
when I bring a sock to be darned
or a book to be mended. Or to my father
as she bustles around the kitchen,
"You're going to have to learn to cook
when I'm gone," she says,
& when he growls "Don't talk rubbish, honey,"
she says cheerily "I know what you're thinking,
you're going to get yourself
a cute young floozie when I'm gone."

"I nearly died when I had you," she says.
"Dr. McCready didn't think I'd make it," she says.
"He never said so but I could tell
by the way he looked at me," she says.
"Look at my pot belly," she says.
"That's what you did to me but it was worth it,"
she says. "You were wanted," she says.
"When I told Dr. McCready I was expecting
he put his arms around me & said
'Oh no, Jeannie, you're not,'
& he looked sadly out the window & then said
'Well, we'll do the best we can,
but you're not to have another, you hear,
you be a good girl now & don't have another.'"
& my father sits silently
when she talks like this,
but sometimes she keeps going & asks
why he has not yet bought their burial plot.
"You can put me wherever you want," she says.
"You'll have someone else to go in your double plot,"
she says. "She won't want me," she says,
"she'll sure make you toe the line," she says.
& when they argue, or when she & I argue,
"You can count on one thing," she says.
"You won't have me around much longer," she says.
"You'll be able to have your own way soon," she says.
She holds out her palm & says, "It's right here,
you can look at it," she says. "The fortune teller
was really upset," she says.
"She took me in her arms & said 'You poor thing,'
& sobbed on my shoulder." "I'll never make 50,"
she says.

75. The Arches

The lily of the valley grows behind the fir tree
behind the east corner of the house
beside the standpipe & the garden hose.
Grows in the dark behind the fir tree
& the arch of the honeysuckle.
"Underneath her arches," my father sings
in the bathroom, just loud enough
for me to hear.
The violets grow on the other side of the house
all along the back of the garage.
Bouquets of violets every April & May,
for my grandmother, my gradeschool teachers,
that I pick in the dim light under the branches
of the maple tree. My father
buys a hydrangea for my mother
on their anniversary, & it is supposed to be blue,
or red, & he plants it in the centre of the lawn
& when it blooms it is white, & he says
that this was only the first year, & the next year
it is again white, & so he puts copper sulphate
in the soil around it, & in the third year
it is still white, & he digs it up
& buys a new one, & when the new one blooms
its petals are pale green, & white.

Hummingbirds come every spring
& dance in front of the honeysuckle
over the arches which my father has built
out of old hydro poles & crossarms.
Under the arches I watch the hummingbirds,
smell the honeysuckle, see
the lily of the valley bloom each year
just in time for Mother's Day.
"Underneath her arches," my father sings,
"happiness is there." The Father's Day flowers

are carnations. They grow near the sidewalk where
roses once had grown. The white carnations outnumber
the red carnations, the red carnations
often die in the frost, some white carnations
have red centres, & are they white carnations
or red? "You wear a white carnation
if your father is dead," my mother says, "a red one
if he's alive." Each Father's Day we pick a spray
of white carnations & drive to Vancouver,
to the cemetery where her father is dead,
& she wears one of the white carnations
pinned to her suit collar, & her mother also
wears a white carnation, & my father
drives the car & tries not to look at the flowers,
& sometimes my mother catches him with a pin
& a carnation, halfway down the sidewalk,
& he looks annoyed, & lifts his chin
as if not to see, & keeps moving his body,
as she pins him, toward the end of the sidewalk,

"Underneath her arches," he sometimes sings,
"there dwells a worm." It is dark & damp
under the arches, & toadstools grow there,
& some years even a frog or snake
lives there in the shadows
of the fir tree. & the lily of the valley
is snow white, & I pick her a small bouquet
every Mother's Day because the blooms are so magically
there, on the right morning. & in the summer,
near the front border where the baby's breath returns each year
my father grows rows of glads & zinnias for the cemetery.
Each spring my grandmother comes out & says
the baby's breath is dead, that my father has killed it,
has mistaken it for a weed. & then my father finds its shoots
hidden in a clump of thrift or heather.

Does it ever bloom? The glads always bloom
& we take them to my grandfather's grave.
While my mother & grandmother stand by the grave
& arrange the flowers, I wander
to a nearby section with tiny headstones. "Our Danny,
always alive in our hearts," I read.
"Our Darling Mary, waiting for us all
in that Happy Land," I read.
Beyond these graves is a sculptured arch of laurel,
with a stone bench, beside it a stream.
& when I am tired of reading headstones
I sit there & wait for my father to come for me
whistling or humming.